PYTHON 3 CRASH COURSE.

UNLOCK

YOUR

PYTHON 3 POTENTIAL

- Vishal Singh

ISBN-13:
978-1720305774

ISBN-10:
1720305773

Why I Wrote This Book

I wrote this Python 3 tutorial book because most of the python programming books out there ignore the basics of programming and start teaching python.

Learning to code requires a proper base of programming fundamentals which is usually ignored by most of the books
This book focuses on teaching programming with very basic illustrations taking real-world examples that a newbie can understand and practice.

According to Stack overflow (a forum) 48% of the members don't have any degree related to computer science. That means large number of people want to become self-taught programmer. This book will be helpful to them. This python book is also designed for kids who want to start programming at early ages of their life.

Contents

4

1. About Python

Python is high level programming language designed for general purpose programming. Python 2 & 3 were released on 16 October 2000 and 3 December 2008 respectively.

Why Python 3

Python 3 is one of the most in demand and easy to learn programming language. This makes a large number of universities to teach python as student's first programming language.

As python is high level programming language it is easier to learn and read. Python programming language became popular because of it's simple and easy to read syntax. Python is open source programming language and free to use.
Python has large community and support that means any problem you encounter will already be solve by others.

Python's history

Python was designed by Guido van Rossum as a hobby project during Christmas and gave it name as python because he was a big fan of Monty python's flying circus.

In December 1989, I was looking for a "hobby" programming project that would keep me occupied during the week around Christmas. My office ... would be closed, but I had a home computer, and not much else on my hands. I decided to write an interpreter for the new scripting language I had been thinking about lately: a descendant of ABC that would appeal to Unix/C hackers. I chose Python as a working title for the project, being in a slightly irreverent mood (and a big fan of Monty Python's Flying Circus).

— Guido van Rossum (source: https://en.wikipedia.org/wiki/Python_(programming_lan guage)

It is used by major organizations like Google, Youtube, Nasa, IBM, Mozilla, Dropbox, Yahoo, Quora. It is mainly used for data analysis, artificial intelligence etc. From building websites to database development. It is also used in finance ,games , GUI development.

The core philosophy of Python is as follows

- Beautiful is better than ugly

- Explicit is better than implicit

- Simple is better than complex

- Complex is better than complicated

- Readability counts

2. Introduction to Programming

What Is Programming

Programming is about writing instructions (known as source code) for computer to perform. Instructions are written in special languages unlike human languages. Computer programming is referred as a set of series of instructions one after another.

It is all about taking an idea, breaking it into small pieces of series of instructions.

Well, this is not new concept to you. You have already done it.

Let me give you an example

You are waiting for your friend at a coffee shop, She calls you

She: Hey I am at railway station, I don't know the way to reach there.

Here you got an idea to make directions from station to coffee shop.

You broke down the whole way into small pieces of series of instructions one after another.

Your instructions will be like this

1. Take right from ABC tower
2. Then go straight
3. Turn left from XYZ road
4. Go straight then you will find the coffee shop.

Like the above example, programming is also a set of series of instructions.

Note: If any order of instructions gets changed your friend may reach to an unknown place, so the order of instructions matters in programming as well like the above example.

What Is Programming Language

Programming languages acts as a bridge between us as a human and computer. It is said that programmers write code that computer understand, Well that's not true at all. Computers don't understand anyone of the programming language it understands only machine code. Programmers write instructions in anyone of the programming language then they convert it into machine code using compiler or interpreter according to the type of programming language they are using.

This fact may arise question in your mind why not we write machine code. Well practically that's not possible in real world. Machine code consist of 0 and 1 arrange in specific manner which computer understands.

Mainly there are 2 types of programming language:

1.High level language: High level languages are easier to understand and they are more-close to English language.
For e.g: 'python'.

2.Low level language: Low level language are tough to understand and they are more-close to machine language.
For e.g: 'c'.

Programming languages further can be classified mainly into 2 types

- Compiled language
- Interpreted language

What is compiled programming language

Compiled languages are the languages in which the source code is directly converted into machine code to perform certain task.
For e.g: c, c++, objective-c etc.

We run a program written in a compiled programming language using compiler in the computer. If a bug is found anywhere in the code the program won't run.

You have written a program and want to share it with

your friend Lilu so he can run it in his own computer. You will compile your code into machine code.

Now your friend Lilu can directly run the program using the machine code file that you have sent him. He can run the program without knowing a single piece of code.

What is interpreted programming language

Interpreted languages are the languages in which the source code is not directly executed by the target machine, but instead read and executed by some other program.
For e.g: php, javascript etc.

We run a program written in a interpreted programming language using interpreter in your computer. The interpreter converted the code into machine code line by line as program runs. The program will only stop at the line where a bug is encountered this make it easier to fix bugs in the code.

You have written a program and want to share with your friend Lilu, so you will directly send the code file having the source code. Now he will run the code using the interpreter installed in his computer.

3. Installing Python

Installing python 3 on windows

First go to http://www.python.org/downloads/

1. click download python 3.6.4 (at the time of making this book latest version was python 3.6.4)
2. select run from the pop-up window.
3. Check the below boxes Install launcher for all users(recommended) and Add python 3.6 to PATH.
4. Double click on install now button.(if python detects earlier version of python installed it will show upgrade now instead of install now)
5. After python has installed click close.

Installing python 3 on mac

1) Browse to http://www.python.org/downloads

2) Click on The Button for Python 3

3) Browse to the Downloads Folder when It is completed and launch the installer

4) Follow through the Installer

Installing python 3 on linux

Python 3 and Python 2 comes pre-installed in linux OS. But you have to go download page and install latest python 3 version on your computer.

<u>1. To check which version of python you have installed go to command prompt and type</u>

$ python --version

If Python 3 is not installed, you will need to install Python with your distribution's package manager. The command and package name varies:

On Debian derivatives such as Ubuntu, use APT:

$ sudo apt-get install python3

On Red Hat and derivatives, use yum:

$ sudo yum install python

On SUSE and derivatives, use zypper:

$ sudo zypper install python3

<u>2. Open a command prompt or shell and run the following command to verify that Python installed correctly:</u>

$ python3 –version

3. Let's get started

Opening IDLE

IDLE stands for **I**ntegrated **D**eve**L**opment **E**nvironment. IDLE is an interactive shell which allows you to directly run the commands on the screen or shell.

On windows and mac

Type and search IDLE and click the IDLE application.

On linux

Open command prompt and type python.

15

IDLE interactive shell looks like this

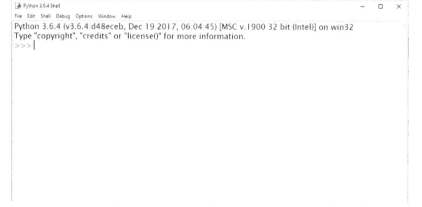

Ignore >>> as it always be there. You can directly code into this interactive shell and it will directly executed here only.

Starting with classical program.

As a ritual a person new to programming is taught to run print hello world code at first. Open python shell and type **print("hello world")** then hit enter. (Make sure you typed including double quotes)

Code 1:

In the interactive shell.

>>> print("hello world")
Hit enter it will immediately run the code.

```
>>> print("hello world")
hello world
>>>
```

Congrats you wrote your first program in python.

Exercise:

print your name
print your best friend's name

Doing maths with python shell.

Numbers are very commonly used in programming world. They are used to represent things like amount of money in your bank account, location of your computer's cursor, time left to avail a discount offer, positions of cars in racing games etc.

Though a good understanding of mathematics can certainly help you to become a better programmer, it is not necessary at start. If you don't have a background in mathematics, try to think of math a way for logical and critical thinking which you will learn as time goes. We will use arithmetic operators '+', '-', '*', '/' to do some basics mathematics like addition, subtraction, multiplication, division respectively.

Type the code after >>> and hit enter.
```
>>> 1+1
2
>>> 7-4
3
>>> 8*5
40
>>> 6/4
1.5
```

Exercise:

1. Find the value of 165482 + 65475
2. Find the value of 544782 - 56395
3. Find the value of 3282 * 65
4. Find the value of 1234 / 2

Solution:

1. 230957
2. 488387
3. 213330
4. 617

Getting started with python text editor

As our code becomes larger and acquires bunch of lines it becomes unfeasible to use python shell to code. Now onward we will be using python text editor to code.

Opening python text editor

Open Python 3 IDLE shell and click **File** located at tool bar.

click **New File** and below mentioned window will pop up.

As we have opened a new file we have to save the file for reuse.

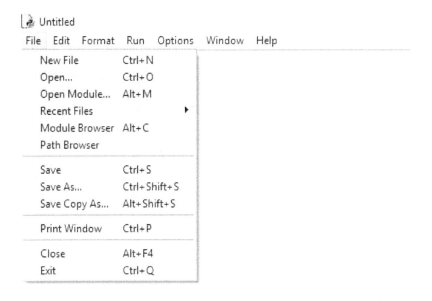

Hit **save** or **ctrl + S** to save the python file.

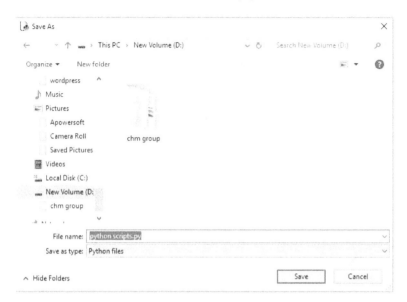

Name the python file whatever you want with **.py extension** and save it.

Type the above hello world program in this text editor.

    print("hello world")

Make sure you have saved the code before running it.

Click the **Run** option in the tool bar and then click **Run Module** it will run the code in the python shell.(As a shortcut first press **ctrl + S** to save the code file and then hit **F5** to run the code)

4. Using print function

Print function will be used almost every time in our program. It is different from the print command which we give while printing documents on paper through printer. print function allows us to print in the python screen i.e python shell as done earlier. We print on python shell by using **print( )** function. We can print any statement like "hello world" or "hii". **print()** is inbuilt function in python. It begins with lowercase '**p**'. Data to be printed on the screen should be enclosed within parentheses '**()**'.

Code 1:

In the python text editor.

print("hello world")

Check the output in python shell.

hello world

This will be the output in python shell.

The quotes are necessary because computers don't understand English language or any other human language. We are specifying the above English sentence in the form of string data type. (we will cover it later)

Code 2:

In the python text editor.

```
print( "first line")

print("second line")

print("third line")
```

Check the output in python shell.

first line
second line
third line

This will be the output in python shell.

If you have noticed that they are in the same order as the source code. Python interpreter reads the source code in the same order as you specific to it.

Let's take look at what python interpreter does with the code we provided. As soon as we hit **Run Module** python interpreter begins to read and interprete the code line by line. In the case of Hello world program python interpreter looks at print function and thinks 'Hmm here is a print function I have to print whatever is enclosed within parentheses into the python shell screen' let's do it now. The words **let's do it now** signifies that python interpreter first reads a code then execute then read then execute line by line.

Exercise:

1. Print what you had today as breakfast .
2. Print your favourite dish.

Solution:
For me
1. Poha
2. Curry rice

5. Variables

What is variable

Variables are like boxes in which you can store items. Variables are used to store information in it. Every variable holds a value, which is the information associated with that variable. We assign data or a value in the variable using assignment operator '**=**'. It doesn't mean 'equal to' like in mathematics. Assignment operator orders python "I don't know what was stored before in this variable but now onwards it will contain what I am assigning now to this variable"

Every variable have it's unique name like lilu, tilu.

For making variable you will need 2 things :

● Variable name

● Some value to store

Code 1:
In the python text editor.

variable_name = 12

Check the output in python shell.

26

You will see nothing happened but in the background a variable with name **variable_name** having value **12** has been stored in the computer's memory. Now you can use this variable as many time as you want.

Code 2:

In the python text editor.

x = 12

print(x)

Check the output in python shell.

12

This will be the output in python shell.

Here we don't need to enclosed variable name **x** within quotes because now your computer identifies 'x' as variable. When it processes the first line, it associates the value **12** with the variable **x**. When it reaches the second line, it prints the value associated with **x** to the screen. Now you can use this variable as many time as you want for stuffs like printing variable etc.

Code 3:

In the python text editor.

x = 12

```
print(x)

print(x)

print(x)

print(x)
```

Check the output in python shell.

12
12
12
12

This will be the output in python shell.

<u>Redefining variables</u>

We can re-defined variable with same variable name. The old data inside the variable will be replaced by new data.

<u>Code 4:</u>

In the python text editor.

```
x = 12

x = 13

print(x)
```

Check the output in python shell.

13

This will be the output in python shell.

Here assignment operator ordered the computer I don't know what x was before but now onward **x** *is variable with data as 13.*

Defining multiple variables in single line

we can defined multiple variables in lines by separating them with comma ' , ' .

Code 5:
In the python text editor.

x,y,z = 12,19,367

print(x)

print(z)

print(y)

Check the output in python shell.

12
367
19

This will be the output in python shell.

Python variable naming

python keywords

We cannot used python keywords in the naming of variables because they are reserved for certain tasks to perform in python

.False	class	finally	is	return
None	continue	for	lambda	try
True	def	from	nonlocal	while
and	del	global	not	with
as	elif	if	or	yield
assert	else	import	pass	
break	except	in	raise	

Python variable naming rules

1. Variable names should not contain spaces.

2. Variables names must start with a letter or an underscore, such as:

    _hello

    hello_

3. The rest of your variable name may consist of letters, numbers and underscores.

ant1

a00b

un_der_scores

4. Names are case sensitive.

Case sensitive means programming language treats uppercase names like ABC and lowercase names like abc different.

case_sensitive, CASE_SENSITIVE, and Case_Sensitive are each a different variable names.

These are the variable naming rules according to python but in real world we have to follow the naming methods followed by the large number of python programmers so that you can work along them in future.

Variable naming conventions

1. Letters in lowercase with underscore if required

shopping_list

selling_list

2. Easy to read names

school_names

my_variable_name

Variable names like **schoolnames** is not practiced naming method because it makes harder to read. So use underscore to make it more readable like **school_names.**

3. Avoid using names with uppercase "I", lowercase "i" and uppercase "O" because uppercase "I" and lowercase "i" looks similar to each other and number 1. And uppercase "O" looks similar to number "0".

4. Don't make variable names descriptive.
no_of_customers_brought_our_product

Exercise:

1. Store some value in variable, and then print that value.

2. Change the value of your variable to a new message, and print it.

6. Comments

Comments are used as similar to an headings we use in our notes. As headings remind us about the topic of the content in the notes. Similarly, comments tell us about why we wrote the piece of code.

In python we use hash mark '**#**' to comment. Anything following a hash mark in your code will be ignored by the Python interpreter. If you write anything after **#** in the line of code editor, python interpreter will ignore the piece of code or anything like a sentence in the English language.

For e.g:

Code 1:

In the python text editor.

#our variables   (this is a comment we used to remind us that the piece of codes below are variables that we defined)

my_variable_1 = 1

my_variable_2 = 2

my_variable_3 = 3

#printing variable

print(my_variable_1)

print(my_variable_2)

```
print(my_variable_3)
```

Check the output in python shell.

1
2
3

This will be the output in python shell.

Code 2:

In the python text editor.

#our variables

```
my_variable_1 = 1

my_variable_2 = 2

my_variable_3 = 3
```

#printing variable

#print(my_variable_1)

```
print(my_variable_2)

print(my_variable_3)
```

Check the output in python shell.

2
3

This will be the output in python shell.

We have comment out the **print(my_variable_1)** so python interpreter didn't interpreted the print command we wrote in the code editor. And output came as **2 & 3** only.
If you want to become a professional programmer or going to work with other programmers, you should write meaningful comments

I'll use comments in the examples throughout this book to help you explain sections of the code.

Exercise:

1. Make 3 variables .

2. Print the value stored in the first and third variable and comment out the second variable.

8.Strings

Strings In Python

In simple words string is a series of characters that you want to display or use in the code. Computers don't understand characters but they understand binary or numbers. Strings are stored in the computer internally in the form of mixtures of zeroes '0' and ones '1'.The conversion of characters into numbers is called as encoding.

We make strings by surrounding them inside the quotes For e.g: my_name = 'kalo'

We have stored the characters **kalo** in the form of string inside a variable named **my_name**.

Making Strings In Python

Strings are made in 3 possible ways:

1.Using single quotes
2.Using double quotes
3.Using triple quotes

Using Single Quotes

As explained in the introduction we make strings by surrounding them inside the quotes. Here we are using single quotes.

Code 1:

In the python text editor.

friend = 'happu'

Check the output in python shell.

It seems nothing happened but in the background we have stored the string inside the variable (discussed earlier in chapter about variables) and now we can use this variable as many time as we want.

Code 2:

In the python text editor.

#making a string and storing inside the variable

friend = 'happu'

#printing the variable

print(friend)

Check the output in python shell.

happu

This will be the output in python shell.

Using Double Quotes

We make strings by surrounding them inside the quotes. Here we are using double quotes.

Code 3:

In the python text editor.

#making a string and storing inside the variable

friend = "happu"

#printing the variable

print(friend)

Check the output in python shell.

happu

This will be the output in python shell.

Using Triple Quotes

Using triple quotes we can make multi-line strings.

Triple quotes are made in two forms

a.   Triple single quotes

b.   Triple double quotes

Triple single quotes:

Code 4:

In the python text editor.

#making a string and storing inside the variable

friend = '''happu'''

#printing the variable

print(friend)

Check the output in python shell.

happu

This will be the output in python shell.

Triple double quotes:

Code 5:

In the python text editor.

#making a string and storing inside the variable

friend = """happu"""

#printing the variable

print(friend)

Check the output in python shell.

happu

This will be the output in python shell.

What does multi-line string mean

Multi-line string is a string having large numbers of characters and they consume multiple lines. Multiple lines can be created by enclosing characters within triple quotes and shifting them to new line by hitting enter key.

For e.g.

Code 6:

In the python text editor.

#making a string and storing inside the variable

friend = '"""hhappjdjvdjvdovfdivfofdoifdv

dkjdgfodoldffpdokgp

fdhdoijvfibjjfobfob

jhflkbjflkbjfolbfjb

vjhvkjfklfdbolfkjgbfog

kjfgkilfjbf;lbkf;'lfhbu'"""

#printing the variable

print(friend)

Check the output in python shell.

**hhappjdjvdjvdovfdivfofdoifdv
dkjdgfodoldffpdokgp
fdhdoijvfibjjfobfob
jhflkbjflkbjfolbfjb
vjhvkjfklfdbolfkjgbfog
kjfgkilfjbf;lbkf;'lfhbu**

This will be the output in python shell.

This same can be done with triple single quotes.

Note: you can use these 3 methods to make string but stick to anyone of the first two methods as they are used by large number of python programmers. I use double quotes to make a string in python. Use triple quotes to make multi-line strings.

Quotes Inside Quotes In The String

Quotes inside quotes means that when we make a string by surrounding characters inside the quotes. It may happen that the string containing characters are quotes. If we use quotes inside the quotes it may

happen that we will get an error or will not get our desired output.
For e.g

Code 7:

In the python text editor.

#making a string and storing inside the variable

x = 'that's like my lilu'

#printing the variable

print(x)

Check the output in python shell.

SyntaxError: invalid syntax

You will get syntax error.

How to solve this problem

If you use single quotes as characters to make string then surround the characters with double quotes or vice versa and alternative method is surround them inside triple quotes.

For e.g

Single quotes as characters in the string enclosing them inside double quotes

Code 8:

In the python text editor.

#making a string and storing inside the variable

x = "that's like my lilu"

#printing the variable

print(x)

Check the output in python shell.

that's like my lilu

This will be the output in python shell.

Single quotes as characters in the string enclosing them inside triple quotes

Code 9:

In the python text editor.

#making a string and storing inside the variable

x = """that's like my lilu"""

#printing the variable

print(x)

Check the output in python shell.

that's like my lilu

This will be the output in python shell.

Double quotes as characters in the string enclosing them inside triple quotes

Code 10:

In the python text editor.

#making a string and storing inside the variable

x = ''' "lilu" '''

#printing the variable

print(x)

Check the output in python shell.

"lilu"

This will be the output in python shell.

Playing with strings

As we know the conventional way of counting in the English language starts with number '**1**' while python uses zero-based index to locate the data stored in the string. This makes little confusion in our mind at the beginning of learning python language.

For e.g

x = " pika chu "

String characters		p	i	k	a		c	h	u		
Index number	0	1	2	3	4	5	6	7	8	9	10

There are white spaces located at the zero '0', five '5', nine '9', ten '10' index numbers in the string.

String characters		p	i	k	a		c	h	u		
Index number	-11	-10	-9	-8	-7	-6	-5	-4	-3	-2	-1

There are white spaces located at the '-11', '-6','-2', '-1' index numbers in the string.

The letters 'p', 'i', 'k', 'a', 'c', 'h",'u' in the string are located at -10, -9, -8, -7, -5, -4, -3 index numbers respectively.

We use square brackets '[ ]' to specify index number.

Code 11:

In the python text editor.

x = " pika chu "

print(x[1])

print(x[0])

print(x[7])

print(x[9])

print(x[5])

print(x[2])

print(x[10])

print(x[3])

Check the output in python shell.

p

h

i

k

This will be the output in python shell.
print(x[0]), print(x[9]), print(x[5]), print(x[10]) gave white spaces in the output while other print commands gave their respective index numbered characters.

The output contains the characters in the same order as we mentioned their index number in the print command.

Slicing Strings

We can slice out characters from the string by using

print(x[0:3])

If we want to slice out characters from index number 0 to 5 of a variable named **x** we have to specify index number inside the square brackets from 0 to 6.
For e.g

Code 12:

In the python text editor.

#making a string and storing inside the variable

x = """that's like my lilu"""

#slicing the characters

print(x[0:6])

Check the output in python shell.

that's

This will be the output in python shell.

Note: If you specify the last index number to slice out till as n you will get characters till n-1 index number.

Converting characters
Converting characters into uppercase(i.e ABC)

We use upper method '.upper()' to uppercase characters in python.

Code 13:

In the python text editor.

#making a string and storing inside the variable

x = """that's like my lilu"""

#making uppercase

print(x.upper())

Check the output in python shell.

THAT'S LIKE MY LILU

This will be the output in python shell.

Converting characters into lowercase (i.e abc)

We use lower method '.lower()' to lowercase characters in python.

Code 14:

In the python text editor.

#making a string and storing inside the variable

x = "'THAT'S LIKE MY LILU'"

#making lowercase

print(x.lower())

Check the output in python shell.

that's like my lilu

This will be the output in python shell.

Checking The Length Of String

To check the length of the string we use len function I.e
len()
For e.g

Code 15:

In the python text editor.

#making a string and storing inside the variable

x = "THAT'S LIKE MY LILU"

#making lowercase

```
print(len(x))
```

Check the output in python shell.

19
This will be the output in python shell.

Concatenating strings

Concatenation is a fancy name of combining strings but it is different from arithmetic adding. It's often useful to combine strings. For example, you might want to store a first name and a last name in separate variables, and then combine them when you want to display someone's full name:

Code 16:

In the python text editor.

#making a string

```
x = "hello"

y = "world"
```

#concatenating x and y

```
print(x+y)
```

Check the output in python shell.
helloworld

This will be the output in python shell.

Code 17:

In the python text editor.

#making a string and storing inside the variable

x = "alice " (here we added space)

y = "hill"

#adding x and y

print(x+y)

Check the output in python shell.

alice hill
This will be the output in python shell.

Note:Concatenation is different than addition

Code 18:

In the python text editor.

#making a string and storing inside the variable

x = "1"

y = "2"

#adding x and y

print(x+y)

Check the output in python shell.

12

This will be the output in python shell.
Here we got output as 12 because of concatenation.

Code 19:

In the python text editor.

#making a string and storing inside the variable

x = 1

y = 2

#adding x and y

print(x+y)

Check the output in python shell.

3

This will be the output in python shell.

Here we got output 3 because of mathematical addition.

Converting string into integers

we use **int()** to convert into integer.

Code 20:

In the python text editor.

#making a string and storing inside the variable

x = "1"

y = "2"

x,y = int(x),int(y) **#here we have converted string 1 and 2 into integer 1 and 2**

#adding x and y

print(x+y)

Check the output in python shell.

3

This will be the output in python shell.

Converting integer into string

we use **str()** to convert into string.

Code 21:

In the python text editor.

#making a string and storing inside the variable

x = "my age is "

y = 28

y = str(y) **#here we have converted integer 28 into string 28.**

#adding x and y

print(x+y)

Check the output in python shell.

my age is 28

This will be the output in python shell.

Adding Whitespace to Strings with Tabs or Newlines

In programming, whitespace refers to any non printing character, such as spaces, tabs, and end-of-line symbols. You can use whitespace to organize your output so it's easier for users to read.

Adding Whitespace to Strings with Tabs

\t is the reserved symbol in python is used for **TAB** space. It means where ever we are going to use it in our program it will create a horizontal tab space between. It's the property of the text editor to decide what should be the width of a tab space. Generally a tab space is 4 spaces wide.

Code 21:

In the python text editor.

#tab

```python
print("Name:\t(your name here)")
```

Check the output in python shell.

Name: (your name here)

This will be the output in python shell.

Adding Whitespace to Strings with Newlines

\n is the escape character in Python. It is mainly used to show the output on the new line. **\n** can be used within a string and it will start a new line if typed.

Code 22:

In the python text editor.

#Newline

```python
print("Languages:\nPython\nC\nJavaScript")
```

Check the output in python shell.

Languages:

Python

C

JavaScript

This will be the output in python shell.

Stripping Whitespace

Extra whitespace can be confusing in your programs. For example, if you made a sign up form for a website consisting of username, email for input by the user. It may happen that user submitted his/her username consist of unnecessary whitespaces like **sunny   grill.** And next time when user tries to login with username like sunny grill he/she will get invalid username message . So to avoid this confusion we are going to strip unnecessary whitespaces from the input provided by the user. Python can look for extra whitespace on the right and left sides of a string.To ensure that no whitespace exists at the right end, left end and both end of a string, use the **.rstrip(), .lstrip() & .strip()** method respectively.

Using **.rstrip()** to remove whitespace from right end

Code 23 :

In the python text editor.

#strip from right

```
book_name = " Python 3 crash course "
print(book_name.rstrip())
```

Check the output in python shell.

' Python 3 crash course'

This will be the output in python shell.

Using **.lstrip()** to remove whitespace from left end

Code 24 :

In the python text editor.

#strip from left

```
book_name = " Python 3 crash course "
print(book_name.lstrip())
```

Check the output in python shell.

'Python 3 crash course '

This will be the output in python shell.

Using **.strip()** to remove whitespace from both end

Code 25 :

In the python text editor.

#strip from both

book_name = " Python 3 crash course "

print(book_name.strip())

Check the output in python shell.

'Python 3 crash course'

This will be the output in python shell.

However, it is only temporarily removed. If you print the value of **book_name** again, you can see that the string looks the same as when it was entered, including the extra whitespace. To remove the whitespace from the string you have to store the stripped value back to the variable.

Code 26 :

In the python text editor.

#strip from both

book_name = " Python 3 crash course "

book_name = book_name.strip()

print(book_name)

Check the output in python shell.

 'Python 3 crash course'

This will be the output in python shell.

Exercise:

1. Store a person's name in a variable, and print a message to that   person like hello vishal would you like to learn some python from python 3 crash course.

2. Ask something of your choice from the closest person near you like would you like to learn some python? then print the reply in direct speech like Alice says, "I would love to learn python."

3. Store a person's name in a variable, and then print that person's name in lowercase and uppercase.

4. Slice out the reply you got from your closest person for 2 problem of this exercise as in my case I printed Alice says, "I would love to learn python." I'm going to slice out now as "I would love to learn python."

For e.g:

In the python text editor.

x = ' Alice says,"I would love to learn python." '
print(x[12:-1])

Check the output in python shell.

"I would love to learn python."

5. Check the length of the above output for me the length is 31.

For e.g:

In the python text editor.

```
x = ' Alice says,"I would love to learn python."
'
x = x[12:-1]
print(len(x))
```

Check the output in python shell.

31

6. Print statement like the length of x variable is 31.(make sure you convert integer into string while string concatenation)

for e.g

In the python text editor.

```
x = ' Alice says,"I would love to learn python." '
x = x[12:-1]
x = len(x)
#converting integer 31 into string 31
x =str(x)
y = "the length of the string is "
#string concatenation
```

```
z = y+x
print(z)
```

Check the output in python shell.

7. Strip out whitespaces from right end,left end then both ends of variable x = ' Alice says,"I would love to learn python." '

8. Insert one tab space between comma (,) and double quotes (") and escape the characters after word 'to' to a newline of the above variable then print it.

7. Common Data Types in Python

1. Numeric data types

a. Integer:

Integer is symbolically represented as "int" . They can be negative or positive with no decimal point.
For eg. 2, -4, 9, 156.

To check the data type we use **type( )** *function.*

Code 1:

In the python text editor.

 # variable
x = 2

 # checking the data type
print(type(x))

Check the output in python shell

<class 'int'>

This will be the output in the shell.

b. Float:

Float is symbolically represented as "float". They represent real number with decimals
For eg. 2.0, 4.2, 6.0, 186.9.

To check data type we use **type( )** *function.*

In the python text editor.

Code 2:

 # variable
x = 2.0

 # checking the data type
print(type(x))

Check the output in python shell

<class 'float'>

This will be the output in the shell.

2. Python 3 strings:

String is symbolically represented as "str". Strings are set of unicode characters. We can use single ['string']or double ["string"] quotes to make a string.

For multi-line string we use triple single or double quotes
["""string""" or '''string''']
For eg. "Hello world" ,'hello world'.

To check the data type we use **type( )** *function.*

Code 3:

In python text editor.
 # variable
x = "hi, I am string "

 # checking the data type
print(type(x))

Check the output in python shell

<class 'str'>

This will be the output in the shell.

3.python booleans

Booleans are symbolically represented as 'bool'.They can be either true or false.

There are 2 type of booleans:

•True

In python the significance of True is same as that of English language.
It signifies that a certain condition is true or not.

Note: the letter 't' in True boolean should be in uppercase(i.e. ABC) like True.
Example:

3>2 is True, 4>1 is True.

● False

In python the significance of False is same as that of English language.
It signifies that a certain condition is false or not.

Note: the letter 'f' in False boolean should be in uppercase(i.e. ABC) like False.

Example:
2>3 is False, 1>4 is False.

checking the boolean value of certain conditions.

Code 4:

In python text editor.
 # variable

x = 4>1

 # checking the boolean value

print(x)

Check the output in python shell

True

This will be the output in python shell

To check the data type we use **type( )** *function.*

Code 5:

In python text editor.

 # variable

x = 4>1

 # checking the data type

print(type(x))

Check the output in python shell

<class 'bool'>

This will be the output in python shell

This signifies that the data type is a boolean i.e it is either True or False.

Exercise:

1. Print 2 integers, 2 floats in the python shell.

8. Operators

1.Types Of Operators

a. Arithmetic operator

operator	What does it mean
+	Addition
-	Subtraction
*	Multiplication
/	Division

b. Assignment operator

operator	What does it mean
=	It used to specify or assigned value

c. Comparison operator

operator	What does it mean
<	Less than
>	Greater than
<=	Less than or equal
>=	Greater than or equal
==	equal
!=	Not equal

Note: assignment operator '=' and equality operator '==' are not same

Equality operator is used to compare 2 things are equal or identical.
For e.g 2==2 is True

While assignment operator is used to assign value
For e.g x = 2 (here we have assigned value '2' to variable 'x'.)

9. Boolean logic

Checking the boolean value (True or False) for a given condition

Code 1:

In python text editor.

 # checking the boolean value

```
print(2 > 3)
print(3 > 2)
print(9 < 3)
print(7 < 6)
```

Check the output in python shell

False
True
False
False

This will be the output in the shell.

Code 2:

In python text editor.

 # checking the boolean value

print(3 = 3)

Check the output in python shell

SyntaxError: can't assign to literal

This will be the output in the shell.

Code 3:

In python text editor.

 # checking the boolean value

```
print(3 == 3)
print(8 == 4)
print(7 == 7)
```

Check the output in python shell
True
False
True

This will be the output in the shell.

Code 4:

In python text editor.

 # checking the boolean value

```
print(3 != 3)
print(8 != 4)
print(7 != 7)
```

Check the output in python shell

False
True
False

This will be the output in the shell.

Code 5:

In python text editor.

 # checking the boolean value

```
print(3 >= 3)
print(5 >= 4)
print(1 >= 7)
```

Check the output in python shell

True
True
False

This will be the output in the shell.

Code 6:

In python text editor.

 # checking the boolean value

```
print(3 <= 3)
print(5 <= 4)
print(1 <= 7)
```

Check the output in python shell

True
False
True

This will be the output in the shell.

Logical Operators

Logical operators are used for combining multiple conditions into one big condition. We generally use three types of logical operator 'and', 'or', 'not'.

a. and operator

'and' operator used only if we want both the conditions true simultaneously. In 'and' operator we combine two conditions & it will be true only if both the conditions are true simultaneously.
For e.g

A student will pass in the physics subject only If he/she pass in physics paper-1 and physics paper-2 simultaneously.

Code 7:

In python text editor.

checking the boolean value

```
print(True and True)
print(False and True)
print(True and False)
print(False and False)
```

Check the output in python shell

True
False
False
False

This will be the output in the shell.

Code 8:

In python text editor.

checking the boolean value

```
print(8>3 and 6>1)
print(8<3 and 2<5)
print(2==2 and 3==4)
print(4>=8 and 9<=7)
```

Check the output in python shell

True
False
False
False

This will be the output in the shell.

b. or operator

'or' operator is used only if we want anyone of the condition as True .In 'or' operator we combine two conditions & it will be False only if both the conditions are False simultaneously.
For e.g
A student will pass in the physics subject If he/she is pass in physics paper-1 or physics paper-2.

Code 9:

In python text editor.

 # checking the boolean value
```
print(True or True)
print(False or True)
```

```
print(True or False)
print(False or False)
```

Check the output in python shell

True
True
True
False

This will be the output in the shell.

Code 10:

In python text editor.

 # checking the boolean value

```
print(8>3 or 6>1)
print(8<3 or 2<5)
print(2==2 or 3==4)
print(4>=8 or 9<=7)
```

Check the output in python shell
True
True
True
False

This will be the output in the shell.

c. not operator

'not' operator is used if we want opposite boolean value of the condition. In 'not' operator we get not True as False and not False as True.

Code 11:

In python text editor.

checking the boolean value

print(not True)
print(not False)

Check the output in python shell

False
True

This will be the output in the shell.

Code 12:

In python text editor.

checking the boolean value
print(not True or True)

```
print(not (True and True))
```

Check the output in python shell

True
False

This will be the output in the shell.

Code 13:

In python text editor.

 # checking the boolean value

```
print(not 5!=4 or 6==6)
print(not (5!=4 and 6==6))
```

Check the output in python shell

True
False

This will be the output in the shell.

Exercise:

1. Print 2 integers, floats in the python shell.

2. Check the condition: second integer you

printed is greater than first integer and store the boolean value in variable x.

3. Check the condition: second float you printed is greater than first float and store the boolean value in variable y.

4. Apply 'and' operator on variable x and y and store the resultant boolean value in variable a.

5. Apply 'or' operator on variable x and y and store the resultant boolean value in variable b.

6. Apply 'not' operator on variable a and b.

10. Conditional statements

Conditional statements are for decision making. The ability to make decision is essential in computer programming. For instance, user puts correct pin at an ATM it will displayed menu of options. If user puts incorrect pin he will get different response and if it continues to put incorrect pin 3 times his/her card will be blocked.

Python has three conditional statements

1. if statements
2. elif statements
3. else statements

if statements

if statements determines whether the condition is True or False and the code will only run if condition is True. For e.g: a student will pass only if he/she scores more than 40 % in the examination.

if statements structure
if condition :

code to run if condition is True

We write **if** then a **condition** to check followed by a **colon':'** then hit enter the python editor will automatically indent i.e it will shift four characters to the right of next line this process is called indentation. As there is four characters spaces in the next line after colon ':' in the above code structure.

Code 1:

In python text editor.

```
score = 45
if score > 40:
    print("student is pass")
```

Check the output in python shell.

```
student is pass
>>> 
```

This will be the output in python shell.

Code 2:

In python text editor.

score = 35

```
if score > 40:

    print("student is pass")
```

Check the output in python shell.

You will get nothing because the condition is false.

if else statements

If else statement is used when you want to take 2 actions one when condition is true and another when condition is false.

Code 3:

In python text editor.

```
score = 36
if score > 40:
    print("student is pass")
else:
    print("student is fail")
```

Check the output in python shell.

```
student is fail
>>> |
```

This will be the output in python shell.

Here we have removed else statement from being indented by hitting Back Space

Otherwise it will look like this and it will give syntax error when executed.

```
score = 36
if score > 40:
    print("student is pass")
    else:
    print("student is fail")
```

elif statements

else if statements are used when you have to check multiple conditions one after another. Similar to else statements prevent **elif** from being indented by hitting backspace.

For e.g

You what to give grades to the students according to the marks they obtained in the examination.

Students scored more than or equal to 75 marks are given 'A' grade.
Students scored more than or equal to 65 marks and less than 75 marks are given 'B' grade.
Students scored more than or equal to 40 marks and less than 65 marks are given 'C' grade.
Students scored less than 40 marks are given 'F' grade.

Code 4:

In python text editor.

```python
score = 56
if (score >= 75 and score <= 100):
    print("your grade is A")
elif (score >= 65 and score < 75):
    print("your grade is B ")
elif (score >= 40 and score < 65):
    print("your grade is C ")
elif (score < 40 and score >= 0):
    print("your grade is D ")
```

 Check the output in python shell.

your grade is C
This will be the output in python shell.

If-elif-else chain

Often, you'll need to test more than two possible situations, and to evaluate these you can use Python's if-elif-else syntax Python executes only one block in an if-elif-else chain. It runs each conditional test in order until one passes. When a test passes, the code following that test is executed and Python skips the rest of the tests.

Code 5:

In python text editor.

score = 1000


```python
if (score >= 75 and score <= 100):
    print("your grade is A")
elif (score >= 65 and score < 75):
    print("your grade is B ")
elif (score >= 40 and score < 65):
    print("your grade is C ")
elif (score < 40 and score >= 0):
    print("your grade is D ")
else:
    print("invalid score")
```

Check the output in python shell.

invalid score

This will be the output in python shell.

Using input function

Input function is an in-built function that allows users to interact with computer. User input can come in various forms in our case it is via computer keyboard.
The input() function pauses your program and waits for the user to enter some text. Once Python receives the user's input, it stores it in a variable to make it convenient for you to work with.

For example, the following program asks the user to enter some text, then displays that message back to the user:

Code 6:

In the python script editor.

```
user = input("what is your name?:")

print("hello" +" "+user)
```

#input function will take the data whatever user typed through keyboard and save it in variable named user. Print function will print the data provided by the user.

Check the output in python shell.

what is your name?:|
what is your name?:tika
hello tika
>>> |

This will be the output in python shell.

*Here input function took the input I provided to the question **what is your name?** and stored in the variable **user**. In print function we have used the data stored in the variable named **user**.*

Code 7:

In the python script editor.

#using input

```
score = input("what's the score you made?: ")
# convert str into int
score = int(score)
#condition
if (score >= 75 and score <= 100):

    print("your grade is A")

elif (score >= 65 and score < 75):

    print("your grade is B ")
```

```
elif (score >= 40 and score < 65):

    print("your grade is C ")

elif (score < 40 and score >= 0):

    print("your grade is D ")

else:

    print("invalid score")
```

Check the output in python shell.

```
 what's the score you made?:|
```

```
what's the score you made?: 99
your grade is A
>>>|
```

Here I gave input as 99

This will be the output in python shell.

Exercise:

1. Write a program that asks the user how many people are in their dinner group. If the answer is more than eight, print a message saying they'll have to wait for a table. Otherwise, report that their table is ready.

2. Ask the user for a number, and then report whether the number is a multiple of 2 or not.

3. Check the condition is false: second float you printed is greater than first float in the python shell.

4. Write a program that reads an integer from the user. Then your program should display a message indicating whether the integer is even or odd.

5. Write a program that reads an integer from the user. Then your program should display a message indicating whether the integer is positive, negative or zero.

11. Loops

Loops are used to automate certain amount of work by repeatedly executing certain block of code. This saves our time from writing it over and over.

While loop

While loops continues to execute a block of code until provided condition is true. Boolean conditions I.e True, False is the basis on which loop continue to execute the block of code.

How we construct a loop

while condition is true :

    do something over and over

Code 1:

In the python script editor.

while 2 > 1:

    print("hit 'ctrl + c' to stop me if you can")

Check the output in python shell.

hit 'ctrl + c' to stop me if you can
hit 'ctrl + c' to stop me if you can
hit 'ctrl + c' to stop me if you can
hit 'ctrl + c' to stop me if you can
hit 'ctrl + c' to stop me if you can
hit 'ctrl + c' to stop me if you can
hit 'ctrl + c' to stop me if you can
hit 'ctrl + c' to stop me if you can
hit 'ctrl + c' to stop me if you can
hit 'ctrl + c' to stop me if you can

This will be the output in python shell.

Here as the 2 is always greater than 1 the provided condition will always be True. As the condition is always True while loop will continue run the code over and over. I have printed **hit 'ctrl + c' to stop me if you can** *statement to show you how to terminate an infinite loop.*

The above code will continue to print the provided statement infinite times. What if we want to type a statement 5 times. We have to control the power of while loop as it will continue to execute the code until the condition is true. We will do so by making condition to change at each time when provided code is executed.

Code 2:
In the python script editor.

```
x = 0

while x < 5 :

    print("hello my friend ")

    x = x + 1 # it increase the value at each time by one
```

Check the output in python shell.

hello my friend
hello my friend
hello my friend
hello my friend
hello my friend

This will be the output in python shell.

The variable x gets increased at every time the code is run. While loops continues to execute a block of code until provided condition is true. When x becomes equal to 5 the condition of while loop no longer remains True so while loop deactivates.

Printing numbers from 1 to 20 through while loop

Code 3:
In the python script editor.

```
x = 1

while x <= 20 :
```

```
    print(x)

    x = x + 1
```

Check the output in python shell.

1
2
3
4
5
6
7
8
9
10
11
12
13
14
15
16
17
18
19
20

This will be the output in python shell.

For loop

The **for loop** takes a item from the collection of items in the sequence and executes a block of code once for each item in the collection. For loop iterate through list, strings etc. For loop are used when we know how many times we want to execute the loop.

In python we make for loops as follows:

for [iterating variable] in [sequence]:

    [do something]

Iterating variable is assigned values from sequence one by one until the sequence ends.

Code 4:

In the python script editor.

```
for i in "string":

    print(i)
```

Check the output in python shell.

s
t
r
i
n
g

This will be the output in python shell.

Here the variable **i** is assigned values from the sequence **string** one by one. Then the code in the **for loop** uses the value to print.

Printing hello 5 times using for loop

Code 5:

In the python script editor.

for i in "12345":

   print("hello")

Check the output in python shell.

hello
hello
hello
hello
hello

This will be the output in python shell.

Here the iterating variable is assigned values from 5 charactered sequence **12345** but it didn't used that value instead printed hello. As there were 5 characters in the sequence it printed hello 5 times.

Break and continue statements

Break

To exit a while loop immediately without running the following code in the loop, regardless of any conditional test, use the break statement. The break statement regulates the flow of the loop. The break statement is used to break from the loop at any point. For example:

Code 6:

In the python text editor.

x = 1

while x <= 20 :

   print(x)

   break

   x = x + 1

Check the output in python shell.

1

This will be the output in python shell.

As soon as python interpreter encounters break statement in the loop it exits from the loop, after that it never go back to check the condition in the loop.

Continue

When the continue statement is encountered, python interpreter skips the rest of the code and get back to check the condition of the loop again. Instead of breaking out of the loop without running the rest of the code you can use continue statement to get back to the beginning of the loop depending upon the conditional test's result.

For e.g
 consider a loop that counts from 1 to 10 and prints except number **6**.

Code 7:

In the python text editor.

number = 0

while number < 10:

   number = number + 1

   if number == 6 :

   continue

   print(number)

Check the output in python shell.

1

2

3

4

5

7

8

9

10

This will be the output in python shell.

Exercise:

1. print first 10 odd numbers

2. print first 5 even numbers excluding zero.

12. Data Structures

Lists

Lists are like a container in which other objects are in specific order. The value within the list is referred to as items. Lists are made by enclosing items within square brackets '[]' separated by commas. Lists are normally refers to as collection of related items.

Strings and tuples are immutable while lists and dictionaries are mutable.

What is mutable and immutable.

Mutable means once defined can be re-written. Immutable means once defined cannot be re-written.

We can completely redefined both mutable and immutable by same name.

Code 1:

In python text editor.

my_shopping_list = ["orange","peanuts","rice","banana"]

Check the output in python shell.

Just like strings this list is stored in your computer's memory.

Printing out the whole list

<u>Code 2:</u>

In python text editor.

#making a list

my_shopping_list = ["orange","peanuts","rice","banana"]

#printing the list

print(my_shopping_list)

Check the output in python shell.

['orange', 'peanuts', 'rice', 'banana']

This will be the output in python shell.

Accessing elements in the list

Lists are collections of ordered items, you can access the items or elements through their position numbers (index number).

<u>Code 3:</u>

In python text editor.

#making a list

my_shopping_list = ["orange","peanuts","rice","banana"]

#printing the item

print(my_shopping_list[-2])

Check the output in python shell.

rice
This will be the output in python shell.

Slicing out items

Code 4:

In python text editor.

#making a list

my_shopping_list = ["orange","peanuts","rice","banana"]

#slicing items

print(my_shopping_list[0:2])

Check the output in python shell.
 ['orange', 'peanuts']

This will be the output in python shell.

Re-writing the list

Since Lists are mutable we can re-write the list

Code 5:

In python text editor.

#making a list

my_shopping_list = ["orange","peanuts","rice","banana"]

#rewriting the list

my_shopping_list[0] = "onion"

my_shopping_list[-2] = "tomato"

Check the output in python shell.

Here you have added 2 item at '0' and '-2' index numbers.

Code 6:

In python text editor.

#making the list

my_shopping_list = ["orange","peanuts","rice","banana"]

#re-writing the list

```
my_shopping_list[0] = "onion"

my_shopping_list[-2] = "tomato"
```

#printing the list

```
print(my_shopping_list)
```

Check the output in python shell.

['onion', 'peanuts', 'tomato', 'banana']

This will be the output in python shell.
This is our new rewritten list.

Redefining the list

Here we are redefining the list with same name.

Code 7:

In python text editor.

#making a list

```
my_shopping_list = ["orange","peanuts","rice","banana"]
my_shopping_list = ["mango","potato","dal","ginger"]
```

#printing the list

```
print(my_shopping_list)
```

Check the output in python shell.

['mango', 'potato', 'dal', 'ginger']

This will be the output in python shell.

Concatenating lists

Just like strings we can concatenate lists also.

Code 8:

In python text editor.

#making a list

x = ["orange","peanuts","rice","banana"]

y = ["mango","potato","dal","ginger"]

#concatenating x and y

print(x+y)

Check the output in python shell.

['orange', 'peanuts', 'rice', 'banana', 'mango', 'potato', 'dal', 'ginger']

This will be the output in python shell.

Tuples

Tuples are similar to list except they are immutable that means we can cannot re-write the tuple. In lists we have used square brackets to make list in tuples we use parentheses '()'

Technically, parentheses do not need to be there but it helps python to understand it better. If you want you can put spaces after comma but it doesn't make difference.

Python will order the items of tuple similar to lists in zero-based index.

Printing out the tuple

Code 9:

In python text editor.

#making a tuple

my_shopping_tuple = ("orange","peanuts","rice","banana")

#printing the tuple

print(my_shopping_tuple)

Check the output in python shell.

('orange', 'peanuts', 'rice', 'banana')

This will be the output in python shell.

Getting items by their index numbers

Code 10:
In python text editor.

#making a tuple

my_shopping_tuple = ("orange","peanuts","rice","banana")

#printing the item

print(my_shopping_tuple[-2])

Check the output in python shell.

rice
This will be the output in python shell.

Slicing out items

Code 11:

In python text editor.

#making a tuple

```
my_shopping_tuple =
("orange","peanuts","rice","banana")
```

#slicing items

```
print(my_shopping_tuple[0:2])
```

Check the output in python shell.

('orange', 'peanuts')
This will be the output in python shell.

Note: We cannot rewrite the tuple like lists. If you try to rewrite the list you will get error.

Code 12:

In python text editor.

#making the tuple

```
my_shopping_list = ("orange","peanuts","rice","banana")
```

#re-writing the tuple

```
my_shopping_list[0] = "onion"

my_shopping_list[-2] = "tomato"
```

#printing the tuple

```
print(my_shopping_list)
```

Check the output in python shell.

TypeError: 'tuple' object does not support item assignment

Redefining the tuple

Here we are redefining tuple with same name.
<u>**Code 13:**</u>

In python text editor.

#making a tuple

```
my_shopping_tuple =
("orange","peanuts","rice","banana")
my_shopping_tuple = ("mango","potato","dal","ginger")
```

#printing the list

```
print(my_shopping_tuple)
```

Check the output in python shell.

('mango', 'potato', 'dal', 'ginger')

This will be the output in python shell.

Concatenating tuples

Just like string we can concatenate tuples also.

Code 14:

In python text editor.

#making a tuple

x = ("orange","peanuts","rice","banana")

y = ("mango","potato","dal","ginger")

#concatenating x and y

print(x+y)

Check the output in python shell.

('orange', 'peanuts', 'rice', 'banana', 'mango', 'potato', 'dal', 'ginger')

This will be the output in python shell.

Dictionaries

Dictionaries are used to store objects similar to lists and tuples but in dictionaries items are not stored in specific order instead they are stored associate to their keys. Each value in the dictionaries is associated to it's own unique key. A dictionary in Python is a collection of key-value pairs. Each key is connected to its value, and you can use key to access the value associated with that key. A key's value can be anything like a number, a string, a list, or even another dictionary.

How to make dictionaries

Dictionaries is made by enclosing key:value pairs in curly brackets '{}' and separating them with comma.

Code 15:

In python text editor.

#making a dictionaries

```
x = {"orange":"1 kg","peanuts":"2 kg","rice": "10 kg","banana": "3 dozens"}
```
#printing dictionaries
```
print(x)
```

Check the output in python shell.

{'orange': '1 kg', 'peanuts': '2 kg', 'rice': '10 kg', 'banana': '3 dozens'}

This will be the output in python shell.

Accessing Values in a Dictionary

Code 16:

In python text editor.

#making a dictionaries
x = {"orange":"1 kg","peanuts":"2 kg","rice": "10 kg","banana": "3 dozens"}

#printing value
print(x["orange"])

Check the output in python shell.

1 kg

This will be the output in python shell.

Modifying items in a dictionary

Code 17:

In python text editor.

#making a dictionaries

```
x = {"orange":"1 kg","peanuts":"2 kg","rice": "10
kg","banana": "3 dozens"}
```

#modifying items
```
x["orange"] = "5 kg"
```

#printing the new value

Check the output in python shell.

5 kg

This will be the output in python shell.

Adding new items in a dictionary.

<u>Code 18:</u>

In python text editor.

#making a dictionaries
```
x = {"orange":"5 kg","peanuts":"2 kg","rice": "10
kg","banana": "3 dozens"}
```

#modifying items
```
x["apple"] = "4 kg"
```

#printing the dictionary
```
print(x)
```

Check the output in python shell.

{'orange': '5 kg', 'peanuts': '2 kg', 'rice': '10 kg', 'banana': '3 dozens', 'apple': '4 kg'}

This will be the output in python shell.

Removing items from a dictionary

Code 19:

In python text editor.

#making a dictionaries
x = {"orange":"5 kg","peanuts":"2 kg","rice": "10 kg","banana": "3 dozens"}

#removing items
del x["rice"]

#printing the dictionary
print(x)

Check the output in python shell.

{'orange': '5 kg', 'peanuts': '2 kg', 'banana': '3 dozens'}

This will be the output in python shell.

Exercise:

1. Make your own list, tuples, dictionaries.

2. Perform the all above tasks with them.

14. Functions

Functions are used to reuse a bit of code as many as we want. While coding it often happen that we need to certain piece of code many time. To define function we will be using def keyword then comes name of the function followed by parameters enclosed within parentheses (). Parentheses can be left empty or passed arguments as needed.Then after colon we write the code which we are going to use again and again.

Parameters

Parameters are just names used when defining function.
For e.g
In the below code a and b are parameters.

Code 1:

In the python script editor.

```
def compare_number(a,b):

    if a>b:

        print("a is greater than b")

    elif a<b:
```

```python
        print("a is less than b")

    elif a==b:

        print("a is equal to b")

    else:

        print("invalid input")
```

Check the output in python shell.

Here we have defined our own function named compare_number.

Arguments

while reusing the function user feeds data within parentheses and are replaced by arguments.

For e.g
In the below code 1 and 2 are arguments.

Code 2:

In the python script editor.

```python
def compare_number(a,b):

    if a>b:
```

```python
        print("a is greater than b")
    elif a<b:
        print("a is less than b")
    elif a==b:
        print("a is equal to b")
    else:
        print("invalid input")
```

#here we are using the function we defined

```python
compare_number(1,2)

compare_number(2,1)

compare_number(2,2)
```

Check the output in python shell.

a is less than b
a is greater than b
a is equal to b

This will be the output in python shell.

Using return statement

return statement is used in the code of a function to return value after computing. return statement is followed by the value that is computed by the function.

Code 3:

```
def add_num(a,b):
    output = a+b


x = add_num(2,5)
print(x)
```

Check the output in python shell.

None

This will be the output in python shell.
Note: *Here function has **not return value** to x. That's why print(x) gave output as **None**.*

Code 4:

In the python script editor.

```
def add_num(a,b):
    output = a+b
    return output


x = add_num(2,5)
```

print(x)

Check the output in python shell.

7
This will be the output in python shell.

Exercise:

1.   **Make a function which print the values always as uppercase.**

2.   **Make a function which print the values always as lowercase.**

15. Practice Problems

Exercise 1

Create a program that asks the user to enter their name and their age. Print out a message addressed to them that tells them the year that they will turn 100 years old.

Solution:

```
name = input("What is your name: ")
age = int(input("How old are you: "))
year = str((2014 - age)+100)
print(name + " will be 100 years old in the year " + year
```

Exercise 2

Ask the user for a number. Depending on whether the number is even or odd, print out an appropriate message to the user.

Hint: how does an even / odd number react differently when divided by 2?

Solution:

```
num = input("Enter a number: ")
mod = num % 2
if mod > 0:
    print("You picked an odd number.")
else:
```

```
print("You picked an even number.")
```

Exercise 3

Take a list, say for example this one:

a = [1, 1, 2, 3, 5, 8, 13, 21, 34, 55, 89]

and write a program that prints out all the elements of the list that are less than 5.

Solution:

```
a = [1, 1, 2, 3, 5, 8, 13, 21, 34, 55, 89]

num = int(raw_input("Choose a number: "))

new_list = []

for i in a:
        if i < num:
                new_list.append(i)

print new_list
```

Exercise 4

Ask the user for a string and print out whether this string is a palindrome or not. (A **palindrome** is a string that reads the same forwards and backwards.)

Solution:

```
wrd=input("Please enter a word")
wrd=str(wrd)
rvs=wrd[::-1]
print(rvs)
if wrd == rvs:
    print("This word is a palindrome")
else:
    print("This word is not a palindrome")
```

Exercise 5

Make a two-player Rock-Paper-Scissors game. (Hint: Ask for player plays (using input), compare them, print out a message of congratulations to the winner, and ask if the players want to start a new game)

Remember the rules:

Rock beats scissors
Scissors beats paper
Paper beats rock

Solution:

```
print("'Please pick one:
        rock
        scissors
        paper"')
```

```
while True:
    game_dict = {'rock': 1, 'scissors': 2, 'paper': 3}
    player_a = str(input("Player a: "))
    player_b = str(input("Player b: "))
    a = game_dict.get(player_a)
    b = game_dict.get(player_b)
    dif = a - b

    if dif in [-1, 2]:
        print('player a wins.')
        if str(input('Do you want to play another game, yes
or no?\n')) == 'yes':
            continue
        else:
            print('game over.')
            break
    elif dif in [-2, 1]:
        print('player b wins.')
        if str(input('Do you want to play another game, yes
or no?\n')) == 'yes':
            continue
        else:
            print('game over.')
            break
    else:
        print('Draw.Please continue.')
        print('')
```

Exercise 6

Write a program that takes a list of numbers (for
example, a = [5, 10, 15, 20, 25]) and makes a new list of

only the first and last elements of the given list. For practice, write this code inside a function.

Solution:

```
def list_ends(a_list):
    return [a_list[0], a_list[len(a_list)-1]]
```

Exercise 7

Write a program that asks the user how many Fibonacci numbers to generate and then generates them. Take this opportunity to think about how you can use functions. Make sure to ask the user to enter the number of numbers in the sequence to generate.(*Hint: The Fibonacci sequence is a sequence of numbers where the next number in the sequence is the sum of the previous two numbers in the sequence. The sequence looks like this: 1, 1, 2, 3, 5, 8, 13, ...)*

Solution:

```
def fibonacci():
    num = int(input("How many numbers that
generates?:"))
    i = 1
    if num == 0:
        fib = []
    elif num == 1:
        fib = [1]
    elif num == 2:
        fib = [1,1]
```

```
    elif num > 2:
        fib = [1,1]
        while i < (num - 1):
            fib.append(fib[i] + fib[i-1])
            i += 1
return fib
```

16. Conclusion

Finally, you have completed this book. The fact that you have completed this book is testament of your commitment to learn python programming. I have covered the basics of python programming but there will always be room to learn. Keep an eye on more books from VS programmers. The key to becoming a good python programming is practice.

Finally, leave a review on Amazon to make this book better and better I personally read all reviews for my books.

www.ingramcontent.com/pod-product-compliance
Lightning Source LLC
LaVergne TN
LVHW051248050326
832903LV00028B/2640